A
World
of
Propensities

D1581654

Karl R. Popper

A
WORLD
OF
PROPENSITIES

THOEMMES
Bristol

Published in 1995 by

Thoemmes Press
11 Great George Street
Bristol BS1 5RR
England

© 1990 by Karl R. Popper

First published in 1990
Reprinted 1995

ISBN 1 85506 000 0

Printed in England by Hobbs the Printers Ltd., Southampton SO40 3YS

Dedicated
to the memory
of my dear wife,
Hennie

Preface

I am of course not certain whether the two lectures which I here submit to the patient perusal or the possible refusal of my readers are, as I hope, the best I have produced so far; nor is this question, I admit, of any importance. But I wish to convey to my readers that I have worked hard to make them the best, since I myself have, in writing them, been able to learn things of great importance to myself.

I am grateful to have been able to do this in my 87th and 88th year, despite the drawbacks of failing memory.

A shorter version of the first lecture was given on August 24th, 1988 before the World Congress of Philosophy at Brighton, under the chairmanship of Professor Richard Hare. A shorter version of the second lecture was given on June 9th, 1989 before the Alumni of the School at the London School of Economics, under the chairmanship of its Director, Dr I.G. Patel.

I never should have been able to write either of these lectures without the help of my Assistant, Melitta Mew.

Contents

A World
of Propensities:
Two New Views
of Causality

Ladies and Gentlemen,

I shall begin with some personal memories and a personal confession of faith, and only then turn to the topic of my lecture.

It was 54 years ago, in Prague in August 1934, that I first attended an International Congress of Philosophy. I found it uninspiring. But the Congress was preceded by another meeting in Prague, organized by Otto Neurath, who had kindly invited me to attend a 'Preliminary Conference' ('*Vorkonferenz*' as he called it) which he organized on behalf of the Vienna Circle.

I came to Prague with the corrected page proofs of my book, *Logik der Forschung*. It was published three months later in Vienna, and in English 25 years later as *The Logic of Scientific Discovery*. In Prague it was read by two Polish philosophers, Alfred Tarski and Janina Hosiasson-Lindenbaum, the wife of Tarski's friend and collaborator, Adolf Lindenbaum. Janina Hosiasson and her husband were murdered when, 5 years later, the Nazis invaded Poland and systematically exterminated what they described as its '*Führerschicht*': its 'intellectual élite'. Tarski went from Prague to Vienna where he stayed for a year and where we became friends. Philosophically, it was the most important friendship of my life. For I learnt from Tarski the logical defensibility and the power of absolute and objective truth: essentially an Aristotelian theory at which, it appears, Tarski and Gödel arrived, independently at almost the same time. It was first published by Tarski in 1930, whereupon Gödel, of course, accepted Tarski's priority. It is a theory of objective truth – truth as the correspondence of a statement with the facts – and of absolute truth: if an unambiguously formulated statement is true in one language, then any correct translation of it into any other language is also true. This theory is the great bulwark against relativism and

3

all fashions. And it allows us to speak of falsity and its elimination; of our fallibility; and of the fact that we can *learn from our errors,* from our mistakes; and of science as the search for truth. Moreover, it allows us – indeed, it requires us – to distinguish clearly between *truth* and *certainty.* I vividly remember, in spite of my bad memory, some of my conversations in Prague with Alfred Tarski and Janina Hosiasson and I vividly remember her surprise, if not horror, at my rejection of probabilistic induction, a field in which she had been working for several years. She gave me some of her papers to read, and I found them far better and far more responsibly argued than Reichenbach's theory. I decided that I must try to attend to her work with the greatest care and, if possible, find a way of reconciling her results with mine; or else to see whether her arguments could be used to refute mine. I soon found that this was not possible: and that a probabilistic theory of induction would work no better on her lines than on Reichenbach's. Reichenbach, incidentally, was also in Prague; but when Carnap tried to introduce me to him he refused to talk to me or even to shake hands. Of other participants I remember, of course, Otto Neurath, Rudolf Carnap and Philipp Frank, with all of whom I was on very friendly terms in spite of my opposition to the positivism of the Circle. Schlick, I believe, came a few days later. I can no longer remember whether Waismann and Zilsel were present.

In the course of the Preliminary Conference, Reichenbach read a paper on probabilistic induction and I replied. My reply was printed with his paper in the journal *Erkenntnis;* and it was reprinted 25 years later in the English translation of my *Logik der Forschung* (and also in its second German edition) under the title 'On the so-called "Logic of Induction" and the "Probability of Hypotheses"'.

Carnap was then, and for some years afterwards, entirely on my side, especially concerning induction (and also concerning Reichenbach's personal attitude towards me and my book); and when my book was published 3 months later, he not only wrote a most favourable review in *Erkenntnis,* which he and Reichenbach were editing together, but he defended himself and me when Reichenbach published in the same issue a long attack on me and a critical aside against Carnap's review.

Carnap and I had come, in those days, to something like an agreement on a common research programme on probability, based on my *Logik der Forschung;* we agreed to distinguish sharply between, on the one hand, probability as it is used in the probabilistic hypotheses of physics, especially of quantum theory, which satisfies the mathematical 'calculus of probabilities', and, on the other hand, the so-called probability of hypotheses, or their degree of confirmation or (as I now prefer to call it) their degree of corroboration; and we agreed *not* to assume, without strong arguments, that the degree of confirmation or corroboration of a hypothesis satisfies the calculus of probabilities, but to regard this question, in view of my arguments in *Logik,* as open – indeed, as the central problem.

This was the state of our discussion reached in 1934 and 1935. But 15 years later Carnap sent me his new big book, *Logical Foundations of Probability,* and, opening it, I found that his explicit starting point in this book was the precise opposite – the bare, unargued assumption that degree of confirmation is a probability in the sense of the probability calculus. I felt as a father must feel whose son has joined the Moonies; though, of course, they did not yet exist in those days.

However, I still could comfort myself with the consideration that Carnap had not given up truth in its objective and absolute sense, as defended by Tarski. Indeed, he never did.

It is this view of truth that gives Gödel's important results their non-relativistic sense. It also gives my results their non-relativistic sense; despite what many people say.

Ladies and Gentlemen, please take these remarks as an expression of my gratitude to Alfred Tarski and as a confession of faith: of my opposition to relativism and of my 54-year-long adherence to the Aristotelian theory of truth, rehabilitated by Tarski and successfully applied by him and by Gödel to some mathematical problems. And I wish to add to this confession of faith my unshaken conviction that, next to music and art, science is the greatest, most beautiful and most enlightening achievement of the human spirit. I abhor the at present so noisy intellectual fashion that tries to denigrate science, and I greatly admire the marvellous results achieved in our time by the work of biologists and biochemists and made available through medicine to sufferers all over our beautiful earth.

Admittedly, science suffers from our human fallibility, like every other human enterprise. Even if we are doing all we can in order to discover our mistakes, our results cannot be certain, and they may not even be true. But we can *learn* from our mistakes: great scientists have shown us how to turn our fallibility into objectively testable *conjectural knowledge*. They are continuing to do so at this moment.

All I have said so far has been an attempt to introduce myself to you as a valiant lover of science who has the greatest admiration for the marvellous and often true results of science without believing these results to be *certain*. The results of science remain hypotheses that may have been well *tested,* but not *established*: not *shown* to be *true*. Of course, they *may* be true. But even if they fail to be true, they are splendid hypotheses, opening the way to still better ones.

Our theories, our hypotheses, are our adventurous trials. Admittedly, most of them turn out to be errors: under the impact of our tests their falsity may be revealed. Those theories that we *cannot* refute by the severest tests, we *hope* to be true. And, indeed, they *may be true;* but new tests may still falsify them.

This method of bold, adventurous theorizing, followed by exposure to severe testing is the method of life itself as it evolves to higher forms: it is the method of trials and of the exposure and elimination of errors through tests. Just as life conquers new worlds, new lands, the ocean, the air and space, so science conquers new worlds: new lands, the ocean, the air and space. What we aim to know, to understand, is the world, the cosmos. All science is cosmology. It is an attempt to learn more about the world. About atoms, about molecules. About living organisms and about the riddles of the origin of life on earth. About the origin of thinking, of the human mind; and about the ways in which our minds work.

These are great tasks; almost impossible tasks. But scientists have made almost impossible progress in their bold attempts. I have been most fortunate indeed, throughout my life, to witness some of these attempts from a distance and others even from close quarters; and I have sometimes even participated in the adventure, in the fields of quantum physics and biology.

I now come to my central problem – causality and the change of our view of the world. Up to about 1927 physicists, with few exceptions, believed that the world was a huge and highly precise clockwork. Descartes, the great French philosopher, physicist and physiologist, described the clockwork as mechanical: all causation was push. It was the first, and the clearest, theory of causation. Later, from about 1900 on, the world was regarded as an electrical clockwork. But in both cases it was regarded as an *ideally precise* clockwork. Either the cog-wheels pushed each other, or the electromagnets attracted and repelled each other with absolute precision. There was, in this world, no room for human decisions. Our feelings that we are acting, planning, and understanding each other were illusory. Few philosophers, with the great exception of Peirce, dared to dispute this deterministic view.

But starting with Werner Heisenberg in 1927, a great change occurred in quantum physics. It became clear that minute processes made the clockwork imprecise: there were *objective indeterminacies*. Physical theory had to bring in probabilities.

It was here that I had some severe disagreement with Heisenberg and other physicists, even with my hero, Einstein. For most of them adopted the view that the probabilities had to do with our *lack of knowledge* and, therefore, with our state of mind: they adopted a *subjectivist* theory of probability. In opposition to this, I wished to adopt an *objectivist* theory. This led me to a cluster of largely mathematical problems; problems whose allurement remains with me to this very day.

The mathematical theory of probability deals with such things as throwing dice and tossing pennies, or estimating your expectation of life – perhaps for insurance purposes. How probable is it that you will live another 20 years? This has its own little mathematical problems. Thus, the probability that you will live another 20 years from today – that is that you will still be alive in 2008 – increases for most of you every day and every week as long as you survive, until it reaches the probability 1 on the 24th of August 2008. Nevertheless, the probability that you will survive for another 20 years from any of the days following today goes down and down with every day and every week you live, with every sneeze and with every cough; and unless you die by some accident, it is not unlikely that *this* probability will become close to 0 years before your actual death. Of course, you know that 0 is the lowest possible probability and 1 the highest; and that 1/2 is the probability of an event that may happen or, just as easily, not happen, such as in tossing an unbiased coin where the probability of *'heads turning up'* is equal to the probability of *'tails turning up'*, and each of these events has the probability of 1/2.

Mathematical probability theory, as you may know, plays an important role in quantum physics and, indeed, in all sciences. I have worked on at least seven different problems of probability theory since my introduction to the subject at university. And it was only after decades that I came to satisfactory and very simple solutions. One of these solutions was what I call *'the propensity interpretation of probability'*. I published it first only in 1956, after more than 35 years of study. This theory has further grown so that it was only in the last year that I realized its cosmological significance. I mean the fact that we live in *a world of propensities,* and that this fact makes our world both more interesting and more homely than the world as seen by earlier states of the sciences.

Now let me explain briefly *the propensity interpretation of probability.* For this purpose I will go back to the tossing of coins.

The classical theory of probability erected a powerful system upon the following definition: 'The probability of an event is the number of the favourable *possibilities* divided by the number of all the equal *possibilities.'* Thus, the classical theory was about mere *possibilities;* and the probability of the event *'tails turning up'* would be 1 divided by 2 because there are altogether two equal possibilities and only one is 'favourable' to the event 'tails'. The other possibility is *not* favourable to *'tails'.* Similarly, the possibility of throwing an even number smaller than 6 with a perfect die is 2 divided by 6 which, of course, is the same as 1/3. For there are 6 sides and therefore 6 equal possibilities and only two of these possibilities, that is the sides marked 2 and 4, are favourable to the event 'an even number smaller than 6 turning up'.

But what happens if the die is loaded or if the penny is biased? Then, according to the classical theory – say, at the time of Pascal or at the time of Laplace – we can no longer say that the six possibilities of the die, or the two possibilities of the coin, are *equal possibilities.* Accordingly, since there *are* no equal possibilities in such a case, we simply cannot speak here of probabilities in the classical numerical sense.

Of course, Pascal knew that loaded dice had been invented for cheating at gambling. In fact, everybody knew that if you insert in a wooden die a small piece of lead near, say, the face bearing the number 6, then this number will turn up less frequently than it does in throws with a fair die, and so the number on the opposite face will turn up more frequently. There are still the six possibilites; but they are now not *equal* possibilities but *loaded* or *weighted* possibilities; possibilities that may be unequal and whose inequality or different weight may be assessed, possibilities that may indeed be weighed.

It is clear that a more general theory of probability ought to include such *weighted* possibilities. It is even clear that cases of *equal* possibilities could and should be treated as special cases of weighted possibilities: obviously, equal possibilities can be regarded as weighted possibilities whose weights happen to be equal.

So the idea of weighted possibilities is fundamental for a more general theory of probability. It is needed even for a more general theory of gambling, of games of chance. But what is far more important is that it is needed for all the sciences – for physics, for biology, and for such questions as the probability of surviving a certain number of years. These cases are all very different from and more general than those cases of gambling with strictly homogeneous and symmetrically built dice or pennies or roulette wheels.

But there is no insuperable difficulty in this generalization: it is easy to see that in the absence of equal possibilities, we may still be able to say that certain possibilities and probabilities are greater, or weightier, than others, as in the case where a die is loaded.

The main problem that arises is this: Does there exist a method – or an instrument like a pair of scales – that can help us to find out the actual weight of the weighted possibilities? Does there exist a method that allows us to attribute numerical values to possibilities that are unequal?

The obvious answer is: *yes,* a statistical method; *yes,*

provided we can, as in the case of dicing, repeat the situation that produces the probabilistic events in question; or provided (as in the case of sunshine or rain) the events in question repeat themselves, without our interference. Provided the number of such repetitions is sufficiently large, we can use statistics as a method of weighing the possibilities, and of measuring their weights. Or, to be a little more explicit, the greater or smaller *frequency of occurrences* may be used as a test of whether a hypothetically attributed weight is, indeed, an adequate hypothesis. To put it more crudely, we take the frequency of occurrence as measuring the weight of the corresponding possibility, so that we say that the probability of a rainy Sunday in June in Brighton equals 1/5 if and only if it has been found over many years that, *on average,* there will be rain on one out of five Sundays in June. So we use statistical averages in order to estimate the various weights of the various possibilities.

All this is, I believe, simple and straightforward. But the really important points come now.

(1) If what I have said is true – if we can measure the weight of the possibility of '*two turning up*' in throwing a certain loaded die, and find it to be only 0.15 instead of 0.1666 = 1/6 – then there must be inherent in the structure of throws with this die (or with a sufficiently similar die) *a tendency or propensity* to realize the event '*two turning up*' that is smaller than the tendency shown by a fair die. Thus, my first point is that a tendency or propensity to realize an event is, in general, *inherent in every possibility* and in every single throw, and that we can estimate the measure of this tendency or propensity by appealing to the relative frequency of the actual realization in a large number of throws; in other words by finding out how often the event in question actually occurs.

(2) So, instead of speaking of the *possibility* of an event occurring, we might speak, more precisely, of an inherent *propensity* to produce, upon repetition, a certain statistical average.

(3) Now this implies that, upon further repetition – upon repetition of the repetitions – that the statistics, in their turn, do show a tendency towards *stability,* provided all relevant conditions remain stable.

(4) Just as we explain the tendency or propensity of a magnetic needle to turn (from any initial position it may have assumed) towards the north by (a) its inner structure, (b) the invisible field of forces carried with it by our planet, and (c) friction, etc. – in short, by the invariant aspects of the physical *situation*; so we explain the tendency or propensity of a sequence of throws with a die to produce (from any starting sequence) stable statistical frequencies by (a) the inner structure of the die, (b) the invisible field of forces carried with it by our planet, and (c) friction, etc. – in short, by the invariant aspects of the physical *situation*: the field of propensities that influences every single throw.

The tendency of statistical averages to remain stable if the conditions remain stable is one of the most remarkable characteristics of our universe. It can be explained, I hold, only by the propensity theory; by the theory that there exist weighted possibilities which are *more than mere possibilities,* but tendencies or propensities to become real: tendencies or propensities to realize themselves which are inherent in all possibilities in various degrees and which are something like forces that keep the statistics stable.

This is an *objective interpretation of the theory of probability*. Propensities, it is assumed, are not mere possibilities but are physical realities. They are as real as forces, or fields of forces. And vice versa: forces are propensities. They are propensities for setting bodies in motion. Forces are propensities to accelerate, and fields of forces are propensities distributed over some region of space and perhaps changing continuously over this region (like distances from some given origin). Fields of forces are fields of propensities. They are real, they exist.

Mathematical probabilities are measures that take on numerical values from 0 to 1. 0 is usually interpreted as impossibility, 1 as certainty, 1/2 as complete indeterminacy, and values between 1/2 and 1 – say 7/10 – are interpreted as 'more probable than not'.

Physical propensities may be interpreted somewhat differently. The propensity 1 is the special case of a classical force in action: a cause when it produces an effect. If a propensity is less than 1, then this can be envisaged as the existence of competing forces pulling in various opposed directions but not yet producing or controlling a real process. And whenever the possibilities are discrete rather than continuous, these forces pull towards distinct possibilities, where no compromise possibility may exist. And zero propensities are, simply, no propensities at all, just as the number zero means 'no number'. (If I tell an author that I have read a number of his books and have to admit that the number is zero, then I was misleading him: I have read *none* of his books. Similarly, a propensity zero means *no* propensity.) For example, the propensity of getting the number 14 on the next throw with two ordinary dice is *zero:* there exists no such possibility and therefore no propensity.

Forces in the modern sense were introduced into physics and cosmology by Isaac Newton who, of course, had some predecessors who were feeling their way towards this idea, notably Johannes Kepler. The introduction of forces by Newton was a great success, even though it was opposed by those who do not like invisible or hidden or 'occult' entities in physics. Indeed, Bishop Berkeley may be said to have founded the positivist philosophy of science by attacking Newton for introducing invisible entities and 'occult qualities' into nature. And he was followed in this especially by Ernst Mach and Heinrich Hertz. But Newton's theory of forces – especially of attractive forces – had tremendous explanatory power. And it was further developed and extended, especially by Ørsted, Faraday and Maxwell, and then by Einstein, who tried to *explain* the Newtonian forces in their turn by his theory of curved spacetime.

The introduction of propensities amounts to generalizing and extending the idea of forces again. Just as the idea of forces was opposed by the positivist successors of Berkeley, of Mach, and of Hertz, so the idea of propensities is again rejected by some people as introducing into physics what Berkeley had called 'occult qualities'.

Others have accepted my theory of propensities or objective probabilities, but have (somewhat rashly, I think) tried to improve upon it. I had stressed that propensities should not be regarded as properties *inherent in an object,* such as a die or a penny, but that they should be regarded as *inherent in a situation* (of which, of course, the object was a part). I asserted that the situational aspect of the propensity theory was important, and decisively important for a realist interpretation of quantum theory.

But I was criticized by some people who asserted that the propensities of 1/2 and of 1/6 were intrinsic symmetry properties of a coin or a die, and that the propensity for surviving another year, or 20 more years, was an intrinsic property of the constitution of a man's or a woman's body and his or her state of health. And, as a strong argument, one of my critics appealed to the survival tables of the life insurance companies which, admittedly, seem to incorporate this view.

Nevertheless, the view that the propensity to survive is a property of the state of health *and not* of the situation can easily be shown to be a serious mistake. As a matter of course, the state of health is very important – an important aspect of the situation. But as anybody may fall ill or become involved in an accident, the progress of medical science – say, the invention of powerful new drugs (like antibiotics) – changes the *prospects* of everybody to survive, whether or not he or she actually gets into the position of having to take any such drug. The *situation* changes the possibilities, and thereby the propensities.

I think that this is a perfect counterexample, and that no more needs to be said. Nevertheless, the example may be a little amplified. The new invention may be expensive, at least in the beginning, which may make it clear that not only the intrinsic state of health of a person may count but also the state of his purse, or else the purse of a possible health service and, obviously, the quality of its medical men.

Incidentally, in my first publication on propensities I pointed out that the propensity of a penny to fall on a flat table with heads up is obviously modified if the table top is appropriately slotted. Similarly, one and the same *loaded* die will have different propensities if the table top is very elastic rather than of marble, or if it is covered by a layer of sand.

Of course, every experimental physicist knows how much his results depend on circumstances like temperature or the presence of moisture. But some typical experiments measure propensities fairly directly; for example, the Franck-Hertz experiment measures how the propensity of electrons to interact with gas atoms changes almost discontinuously with the rising voltage of the electrons.

The Franck-Hertz experiment, one of the classic experiments of quantum theory, studies the dependence of this interaction on an increasing voltage. As the voltage rises, the intensity of the current of electrons rises slowly and then, suddenly, falls; it rises again slowly to a still higher level and falls again suddenly. This is interpreted as the result of the single electrons reaching, step by step, the discrete excitation states of the gas atoms. Here the change of the voltage – of an external condition – is the decisive independent variable; and the changing propensities of the electrons and the atoms to interact with each other are recorded, as they depend upon the changing voltage.

For this kind of experiment – and many atomic experiments are of this kind – we need *a calculus of relative or conditional probabilities* as opposed to *a calculus of absolute probabilities* as it may suffice for, say, dicing experiments or for some statistical problems (say, life insurance tables).

A statement in the absolute calculus may be written

(1) $p(a) = r$

to be read: 'The probability of the event *a* equals *r*.' (Here *r* stands for a real number, $0 \leq r \leq 1$). This contrasts with the relative or conditional probability statement

(2) $p(a,b) = r$

to be read: 'The probability of the event *a* in the situation *b* (or given the conditions *b*) equals *r*'.

If we are interested in a situation that does not change (or whose changes we may neglect), then we can work with absolute probabilities or absolute propensities, having once and for all described the conditions. Thus, if you state that the probability of *a* (e.g. of a certain kind of radioactive atom decaying within a year) is one hundred times greater than that of *b* (e.g. of another kind of atom decaying), you will assume constant and stable conditions for both *a* and *b* (and not, for example, that one of these atoms is part of a crystal exposed to radiation by slow neutrons).

But in the Franck-Hertz experiment we are interested in the dependence of the propensity upon conditions that change, indeed, in a definite way (with the voltage *slowly increasing*).

One important aspect of the Franck-Hertz experiment which it shares with many other quantum experiments is that, even though the conditions change, we can *measure* the propensities because there are so many electrons involved: for statistical measurement, the large number of electrons serves extremely

well to replace long sequences of repetitions. But in many kinds
of events this is not the case, and the propensities cannot be
measured because the relevant situation changes and cannot
be repeated. This would hold, for example, for the different
propensities of some of our evolutionary predecessors to give
rise to chimpanzees and to ourselves. Propensities of this kind
are, of course, not measurable, since the situation cannot be
repeated. It is unique. Nevertheless, there is nothing to prevent
us from supposing that such propensities exist, and from
estimating them speculatively.

To sum up: propensities in physics are properties of *the
whole physical situation* and sometimes even of the particular
way in which a situation changes. And the same holds of the
propensities in chemistry, in biochemistry, and in biology.

Now, in our real changing world, the situation and, with
it, the possibilities, and thus the propensities, change all the
time. They certainly may change if we, or any other organisms,
prefer one possibility to another; or if we *discover* a possibility
where we have not seen one before. Our very understanding
of the world changes the conditions of the changing world;
and so do our wishes, our preferences, our motivations, our
hopes, our dreams, our phantasies, our hypotheses, our
theories. Even our erroneous theories change the world,
although our correct theories may, as a rule, have a more
lasting influence. All this amounts to the fact that *determinism
is simply mistaken:* all its traditional arguments have withered
away and indeterminism and free will have become part of the
physical and biological sciences.

The theory of motives determining our actions, and the
theory that these motives in their turn are motivated or caused
or determined by earlier motives, etc., seems, indeed, to be
motivated – motivated by the wish to establish the ideology
of determinism in human concerns. But with the introduction
of propensities, the ideology of determinism evaporates. Past
situations, whether physical or psychological or mixed, do not

determine the future situation. Rather, they determine changing *propensities that influence future situations without determining them in a unique way.* And all our experiences – including our wishes and our efforts – may contribute to the propensities, sometimes more and sometimes less, as the case may be. (In spite of the instability of the weather, my wishes do not contribute to 'sunshine tomorrow'. But they can contribute a lot to my catching the flight from London to San Francisco.)

In all these cases the propensity theory allows us to work with an *objective* theory of probability. Quite apart from the fact that we do not *know* the future, the future is *objectively not fixed.* The future is *open: objectively open.* Only the past is fixed; it has been actualized and so it has gone. The present can be described as the continuing process of the actualization of propensities; or, more metaphorically, of the freezing or the crystallization of propensities. While the propensities actualize or *realize* themselves, they are continuing processes. When they have realized themselves, then *they are no longer real processes.* They freeze and so become past – and unreal. Changing propensities are objective processes, and they have nothing to do with our lack of knowledge; even though our lack of knowledge is, of course, very great, and even though a particular lapse may, of course, be an important part of the changing situation.

Propensities, like Newtonian attractive forces, are invisible and, like them, they can act: they are *actual,* they are *real.* We therefore are compelled to attribute a kind of reality to mere possibilities, especially to weighted possibilities, and especially to those that are as yet unrealized and whose fate will only be decided in the course of time, and perhaps only in the distant future.

This view of propensities allows us to see in a new light the processes that constitute our world: the world process. The world is no longer a causal machine – it can now be seen as a world of propensities, as an unfolding process of realizing possibilities and of unfolding new possibilities.

This is very clear in the physical world where new elements, new atomic nuclei, are produced under extreme physical conditions of temperature and pressure: elements that survive only if they are not too unstable. And with the new nuclei, with the new elements, new possibilities are created, possibilities that previously simply did not exist. In the end, we ourselves become possible.

The world of physics is, we have known for some time, indeterministic. It was long regarded to be deterministic. And then, after quantum indeterminism was accepted, indeterminism was usually regarded as affecting only the tiniest bodies, such as radioactive atoms, and only a very little. But this, it turned out, was a mistake. We now know that not only tiny particles are affected but also the probability of chemical reactions, and thus, of classical mass effects. It has now become clear, especially through the findings of the Japanese chemist, Kenichi Fukui, that unoccupied frontier orbitals play an important part in chemical reactions. But these are just unrealized possibilities – presumably empty de Broglie waves. In any case, they are propensities, similar to attractive forces.

Let us have a quick look at chemical evolution. Especially in the evolution of biochemistry, it is widely appreciated that every new compound creates new possibilities for further new compounds to synthesize: possibilities which previously did not exist. The possibility space (the space of non-zero possibilities) is growing. (Incidentally, *all* spaces are possibility spaces.)

And behind this growth there seems to be hidden something like a natural law that can be stated as follows: All non-zero possibilities, even those to which only a tiny non-zero propensity is attached, will realize themselves in time, provided they have time to do so; that is to say, provided the conditions repeat themselves sufficiently often or remain constant over a sufficiently long period of time. This law amounts to stating that there is a kind of *horror vacui* in the various possibility spaces (perhaps a kind of horror of empty de Broglie waves, so that the propensities are like *active* attractive forces).

Just like a newly synthesized chemical compound, whose creation in turn creates new possibilities for new compounds to synthesize, so all new propensities always create new possibilities. And new possibilities tend to realize themselves in order to create again new possibilities. Our world of propensities is inherently creative.

These tendencies and propensities have led to the emergence of life. And they have led to the great unfolding of life, to the evolution of life. And the evolution of life has led to better conditions for life on earth and thus to new possibilities and propensitites; and to new forms of life that differ widely from the old forms and from each other. All this means that possibilities – possibilities that have not yet realized themselves – have a kind of reality. The numerical propensities that attach to the possibilities can be interpreted as a measure of this status of a not yet fully realized reality – a reality in the making. And in so far as these possibilities can, and partly will, realize themselves in time, the open future is, in some way, already present, with its many competing possibilities, almost as a promise, as a temptation, as a lure. The future is, in this way, *actively* present at every moment.

The old world picture that puts before us a mechanism operating with pushes, or with more abstract causes that are all in the past – the past kicking us and driving us with kicks into the future, the past that is *gone* – is no longer adequate in our indeterministic world of propensities. Causation is just a special case of propensity: the case of a propensity equal to 1, a *determining* demand, or force, for realization. It is not the kicks from the back, from the past, that *impel* us but the attraction, the lure of the future and its competing possibilities, that *attract* us, that *entice* us. This is what keeps life – and, indeed, the world – unfolding. (Remember that Newtonian forces too are attractive forces!)

I now turn to *causation.* In the light of what has been said about propensities, two comments will be made on causation; comments that appear to me new.

The first is a comment on the deterministic push theory of causation. In Plato and Aristotle, movement is something that needs an explanation: it is explained by a mover. This idea is clarified and elaborated in Descartes's clockwork theory of the world. The world is a mechanical clockwork in which a cog of one cog-wheel pushes the adjacent cog of the adjacent cog-wheel. Since the wheels are perfect, there is no loss of movement. The first mover is the first cause, and *all causation is push.* Newton was still thinking on these lines and therefore made an attempt, as he hints in the *Optics,* to reduce the attractive pull to push. But in contrast to Lesage, he realized that a theory of the Lesage type would not work. So Descartes's monistic push theory of causation gave way to a *push-me-pull-you* theory: shocking at first, even to Newton himself, but still highly intuitive, even for a poet such as Pope.

Faraday and Maxwell prepared for the electrification of the world-clock. Push is no longer symmetrical with pull, and Ørsted forces play a most important additional role. But these Ørsted forces are not central and therefore they really destroy the intuitive character of the push-me-pull-you world. Physics becomes now abstract: Ørsted forces make a field theory inevitable. And so the new physics was called 'theoretical physics' or '*Theoretische Physik*'; first, I think, in Berlin, in the Helmholtz circle. It tried to describe the abstract, the hidden, the invariant structural properties of the physical world. *Cause* became that state of affairs which, *relative to an accepted theory,* was described by the initial conditions. *Effect* was that event or that state of affairs which the theory, in the presence of the initial conditions, would predict.

Owing to this deductive relationship, it is trivial that, in the presence of the theory, the probability of the effect given the cause equals 1:

$$p \ (effect, \ cause) \ = \ 1$$

This, I say, is trivial. But it leads in our world of propensities to the following view. What may happen in the future – say, tomorrow at noon – is, to some extent, open. There are many possibilities trying to realize themselves, but few of them have a very high propensity, given the existing conditions. When tomorrow noon approaches, under constantly changing conditions, many of these propensities will have become zero and others very small; and some of the propensities that remain will have increased. At noon, those propensities that realize themselves will be equal to 1 in the presence of the then existing conditions. Some will have moved to 1 continuously; others will have moved to 1 in a discontinuous jump. (One can therefore still distinguish between *prima facie* causal and acausal cases.) And although we may regard the ultimate state of the conditions at noon as the cause of the ultimate realization of the propensities, there is nothing of the old Cartesian deterministic push left in this view of the world.

This is my first comment on causation in the light of the theory of propensities. But to complement the first, a second comment is needed.

In our theoretical physics, that is in our somewhat abstract description of the invariant structural properties of our world, there are what we may call natural laws of a deterministic character and others that we may call natural laws of a probabilistic character, like those described by Franck and Hertz. Let us first look at the deterministic laws – say, Kepler's laws, since they are still valid in Einstein's theory for not too excentric planetary ellipses; or, say, Bohr's wonderful 1921 theory of the periodic system.

What is the status of this kind of theory that describes the structural properties of our world?

They are hypotheses, arrived at in (often unsuccessful) attempts to solve some problems such as Kepler's great problem to find the secrets of the *'Harmony of the Universe'*, or Bohr's problem of explaining the periodic system of elements in terms of his theory of the electrons surrounding the Rutherford nuclei. That they were wonderful hypotheses, I wish to stress, in full admiration of the great achievement of these masters. Yet that they were not more than hypotheses we know from the fact that Kepler's laws were corrected by Newton and Einstein, and that Bohr's theory was corrected by the theory of isotopes.

Being hypotheses, these theories had to be tested. And it was the close agreements with the tests that gave them their great importance.

Now, how are such theories tested? Obviously by making experiments. And this means: *by creating, at will, artificial conditions that either exclude, or reduce to zero, all the interfering and disturbing propensities.*

Only the system of our planets is so well isolated from all extraneous mechanical interference that it is a unique, natural laboratory experiment. Here, only the *internal* disturbances interfere with the precision of Kepler's laws. Kepler knew nothing of these problems, for example of the insolubility of the three-body problem, and it was one of the glories of Newton's theory that he invented an approximation method of solving them. He tamed, up to a point, the disturbing propensities of the planets for interfering with each other.

In most laboratory experiments we have to exclude many disturbing extraneous influences such as changes of temperature or the normal moisture of the air. Or we may have to create an artificial environment of extreme temperatures – say, near to absolute zero. In this we are led entirely by our hypothetical insight into the theoretical structure of our world. And we have to learn from our experimental mistakes that lead to unsatisfactory results: results are satisfactory only if they can be repeated at will; and this happens only if we have learnt how to exclude the interfering propensities.

But what does all this show us? It shows that in the non-laboratory world, with the exception of our planetary system, no such strictly deterministic laws can be found. Admittedly, in certain cases such as the planetary movements, we can interpret events as due to the vectorial sum of forces that our theories have isolated. But in any actual event such as, say, the fall of an apple from a tree, this is not the case. Real apples are emphatically not Newtonian apples. They fall usually when the wind blows. And the whole process is initiated by a biochemical process that weakens the stem so that the often-repeated movement due to the wind, together with the Newtonian weight of the apple, leads to a snap of the stem – a process that we can analyse but cannot calculate in detail, mainly because of the probabilistic character of the biochemical processes that prevents us from predicting what will happen in a unique situation. What we might be able to calculate is the propensity of a special type of apple to fall within, say, the next hour. This *may* make it possible for us to predict that, if the weather deteriorates, it will very probably fall within the next week. There is no determinism in Newton's falling apple if we look at it realistically. And much less in many of our changing states of mind, for example in our so-called motives. Our inclination to think deterministically derives from our acts as movers, as pushers of bodies: from our Cartesianism. But today this is no longer science. It has become ideology.

All this is now supported by the new results of the mathematics of dynamic (or deterministic) chaos.

This new theory has shown that, even on the assumption of a classical (or 'deterministic') system of mechanics, we may obtain, from some special but quite simple initial conditions, motions that are 'chaotic', in the sense that they quickly become completely *unpredictable*. As a consequence, we can now easily explain such facts within classical 'deterministic' physics as the molecular chaos of every gas. We neither need to *assume* them, nor do we need to call upon quantum physics for their derivation.

This argument seems to me valid. But an interpretation that is sometimes linked with it seems to me invalid. It says that we may − or that we should − assume that our world is in reality deterministic, even where it appears to be indeterministic or chaotic; that behind an indeterministic appearance, there lies hidden a deterministic reality. This interpretation I regard as a mistake. For what has been established is that classical physics is only seemingly (or *prima facie*) deterministic; that its determinism fits only problems of a special kind, such as the Newtonian two-body problem, while it turns out to be indeterministic if problems of a wider range are taken into consideration. (This view I have upheld at least since 1950; compare my paper 'Indeterminism in Quantum Physics and in Classical Physics' (BJPS 1950) and my book, *The Open Universe* (1982) with an interpretation of some important results by Hadamard.)

To sum up, neither our physical world nor our physical theories are deterministic, even though of course many possibilities are excluded by the laws of nature and of probability: there are many zero propensities. And even non-zero propensities that are very small will not realize themselves if the situation changes before they had a chance. The fact that conditions are never quite constant may, indeed, explain why certain very low propensities seem never to realize themselves. Shaking the beaker in dicing is intended to make the throws independent of each other. But it may indeed do more: it may disturb that constancy of the physical conditions which is a mathematical condition for very low propensities to realize themselves. This may perhaps explain the claim of some experimenters that *a priori* extremely improbable runs occur in fact even less often than they should according to theory. We cannot ensure that all the probabilistically relevant conditions are really kept constant.

The future is open. It is especially obvious in the case of the evolution of life that the future always was open. It is obvious that in the evolution of life there were almost infinite possibilities. But they were largely exclusive possibilities; so most steps were exclusive choices, destroying many possibilities. As a consequence, only comparatively few propensities could realize themselves. Still, the variety of those that have realized themselves is staggering. I believe that this was a process in which both *accidents* and *preferences,* preferences of the organisms for certain possibilities, were mixed: the organisms were in search of a better world. Here the preferred possibilities were, indeed, allurements.

Looking at my own long life, I find that the main allurements which led me on and on from my 17th year were *theoretical problems*. And among these the problems of science and of probability theory loomed large. These were *preferences*. The solutions were *accidents*.

A brief closing passage from the preface to a book of mine may apply all this to the education of young scientists.

I think that there is only one way to science – or to philosophy, for that matter: to meet a problem, to see its beauty and fall in love with it; to get married to it and to live with it happily, till death do ye part – unless you should meet another and even more fascinating problem or unless, indeed, you should obtain a solution. But even if you do obtain a solution, you may then discover, to your delight, the existence of a whole family of enchanting, though perhaps difficult, problem children, for whose welfare you may work, with a purpose, to the end of your days.

Towards an Evolutionary
Theory of Knowledge

My dear Director, Ladies and Gentlemen,

In 1944 I was travelling with my wife in a bitterly cold bus, returning from a skiing holiday on Mount Cook. The bus stopped in the middle of nowhere, at a snowed-in rural New Zealand post office. To my surprise, I heard my name called, and someone handed me a telegram – the telegram that changed our lives. It was signed F.A. Hayek, and it offered me a Readership at the London School of Economics. The appointment followed in 1945, and in 1949 I was given the title of Professor of Logic and Scientific Method.

Today's lecture to the Alumni of the School, for which you, Dr Patel, so kindly invited me, is the first public lecture I have ever been asked to give at the L.S.E. I hope, Dr Patel, that you will allow me to regard it, quite informally, as my slightly belated Inaugural Address. It is an occasion to which I have been looking forward eagerly for the last 40 years.

My second request to you, dear Dr Patel, is to allow me to change the wording of the title of this address. When I was urged by the School to produce a title, I had little time to think. I now feel that 'Evolutionary Epistemology' sounds pretentious, especially since there exists a less pretentious equivalent. So, please let me change my title to its equivalent and let me call this Inaugural Address 'Towards an Evolutionary Theory of Knowledge'.

It is my aim, and my problem, at this Inaugural to interest you in work done and, even more, in work yet to be done in the theory of knowledge, by placing it in the wide and exciting context of biological evolution, and to show you that we can learn something new from such an exercise.

I do not start by asking a question such as 'What is knowledge?' and, even less, 'What does "knowledge" mean?'. Instead, my starting point is a very simple proposition – indeed, an almost trivial one – the proposition *that animals can know something: that they can have knowledge*. For example, a dog may know that his master returns home, on working days, at about 6 p.m., and the behaviour of the dog may give many indications, clear to his friends, that he expects the return of his master at that time. I shall show that, in spite of its triviality, the proposition that *animals can know something* completely revolutionizes the theory of knowledge as it is still widely taught.

There are, of course, some people who would deny my trivial proposition. They might say, perhaps, that in attributing knowledge to the dog I am merely using a metaphor, and a blatant anthropomorphism. Even biologists interested in the theory of evolution have said such things. My reply is: yes, it is a blatant anthropomorphism, but it is not merely a metaphor. And the anthropomorphism is a very useful one: one that is indispensable in any theory of evolution. If you speak of the nose of the dog, or of his legs, then these are also anthropomorphisms, even though we take for granted that it is simply true that the dog has a nose – if somewhat different from our human nose.

Now, if you are interested in the theory of evolution, you will find that part of it is the important theory of homology, and that the dog's nose and my nose are homologous, which means that they are both inherited from a distant common ancestor. Without this hypothetical theory of homology, evolutionary theory could not exist. Obviously, the theory of homology is a highly speculative and very successful hypothesis, and one that all evolutionists adopt. My attribution of knowledge to the dog is therefore an anthropomorphism, but it is not just a metaphor. Rather, it implies the hypothesis that some organ of the dog, in this case presumably the brain, has a function that corresponds not only in some vague sense to the biological function of human knowledge, but is homologous with it.

Please note that the things that may be homologous are, in the original sense, organs. But they may also be functions of organs. And they may also be procedures. Even behaviour may be hypothesized to be homologous in the evolutionary sense; for example, courtship behaviour, especially ritualized courtship behaviour. That this is indeed homologous in the hereditary or genetic sense between, say, different but closely related species of birds, is very convincing. That it is homologous between ourselves and some species of fish seems highly dubious, yet it remains a serious hypothesis. Of course, the possession of a mouth or of a brain in fish is most convincingly homologous with our possession of the corresponding organs: it is quite convincing that they are genetically derived from the organs of a common ancestor.

I hope the central importance of the theory of homology for the theory of evolution has become sufficiently clear for my purpose; that is, for defending the existence of animal knowledge, not as a mere metaphor, but as a serious evolutionary hypothesis.

This hypothesis does in no way imply that animals will be aware of their knowledge; and it thereby draws attention to the fact that we ourselves possess knowledge of which we are not aware, not conscious.

Our own unconscious knowledge has often the character of unconscious *expectations*, and sometimes we may become conscious of having had an expectation of this kind when it turns out to have been mistaken.

An example of this is an experience that I had several times in my long career: in going down some stairs and reaching the last step, I almost fell, and became aware of the fact that I had unconsciously expected that there was one more step, or one less step, than actually existed.

This led me to the following formulation: when we are surprised by some happening, the surprise is usually due to an unconscious *expectation* that something else would happen.

I shall now try to give you a list of 19 interesting conclusions that we can draw, and partly have drawn (although so far unconsciously) from our trivial proposition that animals can know something.

1. Knowledge has often the character of expectations.

2. Expectations have usually the character of hypotheses, of conjectural or hypothetical knowledge: they are *uncertain*. And those who expect, or who know, may be quite unaware of this uncertainty. In the example of the dog, the dog may die without ever having been disappointed in this expectation of his master's timely return: but *we* know that the timely return was never certain, and that the dog's expectation was a very risky hypothesis. (After all, there might have been a railway strike.) So we can say:

3. Most kinds of knowledge, whether of men or animals, are hypothetical or conjectural; especially the very ordinary kind of knowledge, just described as having the character of an expectation; say, the expectation, supported by a printed official timetable, that at 5.48 p.m. there will arrive a train from London. (In some libraries, embittered or merely discerning readers returned timetables to the shelves headed 'Fiction'.)

4. In spite of its uncertainty, of its hypothetical character, much of our knowledge will be objectively *true*: it will correspond to the objective *facts*. Otherwise we could hardly have survived as a species.

5. We therefore must clearly *distinguish* between the *truth* of an expectation or a hypothesis and its *certainty*; and therefore between two ideas: *the idea of truth* and *the idea of certainty*; or, as we may also say, between *truth* and *certain truth* – for example, a mathematically demonstrable truth.

6. There is much truth in much of our knowledge, but little certainty. We must approach our hypotheses *critically*; we must test them as severely as we can, in order to find out whether they cannot be shown to be false after all.

7. Truth is objective: it is correspondence to the facts.

8. Certainty is rarely objective: it is usually no more than a strong feeling of trust, of conviction, although based on insufficient knowledge. Such feelings are dangerous since they are seldom well-founded. Strong feelings of conviction make dogmatists of us. They may even turn us into hysterical fanatics who try to convince themselves of a certainty which they unconsciously know is not available.

Before proceeding with this list to the next point (to point 9.), I wish to digress for a moment. For I want to say a few words against the widespread doctrine of sociological relativism, often unconsciously held, especially by sociologists who study the ways of scientists and who think that they thereby study science and scientific knowledge. Many of these sociologists do not believe in objective truth, but think of truth as a sociological concept. Even a former scientist such as the late Michael Polanyi thought that truth was what the experts *believe* to be true – or, at least, the great majority of the experts. But in all sciences, the experts are sometimes mistaken. Whenever there is a breakthrough, a really important new discovery, this means that the experts have been proved wrong, and that the facts, the objective facts, were different from what the experts expected them to be. (Admittedly, a breakthrough is not a frequent event.)

I do not know of any creative scientist who has made no mistakes; and here I am thinking of the very greatest – Galileo, Kepler, Newton, Einstein, Darwin, Mendel, Pasteur, Koch, Crick, and even Hilbert and Gödel. Not only all animals are fallible, but also all men. So there are experts, but no authorities – a fact that has not yet established itself sufficiently. Of course, we are all very conscious of the fact that we ought not to make mistakes, and we all try very hard. (Perhaps Gödel tried harder than anyone else.) But still, we are fallible animals – fallible mortals, as the early Greek philosophers would have it: only the Gods can know, we mortals can only opine and guess.

I guess, indeed, that it is the suppressed sense of our own fallibility that is responsible for our despicable tendency to form cliques and to go along with whatever seems to be fashionable: that makes so many of us howl with the wolves. All this is human weakness, which means it ought not to exist. But it does exist, of course; it is even to be found among some scientists. And as it exists, we ought to combat it; first in ourselves, and then, perhaps, in others. For I hold that science *ought* to strive for objective truth, for truth that depends only on the facts; on truth that is above human authority and above arbitration, and certainly above scientific fashions. Some sociologists fail to understand that this objectivity is a possibility towards which science (and therefore scientists) should aim. Yet science *has* aimed at truth for at least 2,500 years.

But let us now return to our evolutionary theory of knowledge, to our trivial starting proposition that animals can know something, and to our list of results obtained from, or suggested by, this trivial proposition.

9.   Can only animals know? Why not plants? Obviously, in the biological and evolutionary sense in which I speak of knowledge, not only animals and men have expectations and therefore (unconscious) knowledge, but also plants; and, indeed, all organisms.

10.   Trees know that they may find much-needed water by pushing their roots into deeper layers of the earth; and they know (or the tall ones do) how to grow up vertically. Flowering plants know that warmer days are about to arrive, and they know how and when to open their flowers, and to close them – according to sensed changes in radiation intensity or in temperature. Thus they have something like sensations or perceptions to which they respond, and something like sense organs. And they know, for example, how to attract bees and other insects.

11.   An apple tree that sheds its fruit or its leaves offers a beautiful example for one of the central points of our investigations. The tree is adapted to the seasonal changes of the year. Its structure of inbuilt biochemical processes keeps them in step with these law-like and long-term environmental changes. It expects these changes: it is attuned to them, it has foreknowledge of them. (Trees, especially tall trees, are also finely adjusted to such invariants as gravitational forces.) But the tree responds, in an appropriate and well-adapted manner, also to short-term changes and forces, and even to momentary events in the environment. Chemical changes in the stems of the apples and of the leaves prepare them for falling; but they usually fall in response to the momentary pull of the wind: the ability to respond appropriately to short-term or even momentary events or changes in the environment is closely analogous to the ability of an animal to respond to short-term perceptions, to sense experiences.

12.   The distinction between adaptation to, or (unconscious) knowledge of, law-like and long-term environmental conditions, such as gravity and the cycle of

the changing seasons, on the one side, and adaptation to, or knowledge of, environmental short-term changes and events, on the other side, is of the greatest interest. While short-term events occur in the life of the individual organisms, the long-term and law-like environmental conditions are such that adaptation to them must have been at work throughout the evolution of countless generations. And if we look more closely at short-term adaptation, at the knowledge of, and the response to, environmental short-term events, then we see that the *ability* of the individual organism to respond appropriately to short-term events (such as a particular pull of the wind or, in the animal kingdom, the appearance of a foe) is also a long-term adaptation, and also the work of adaptation going on through countless generations.

13.   A grazing flock of wild geese is approached by a fox. One of them sees the fox and gives the alarm. It is precisely a situation like this – a short-term event – in which the eyes of an animal can save its life. The animal's ability to respond appropriately depends on its possession of eyes – of sense organs – adapted to an environment in which daylight is periodically available (analogous to the change of the seasons or of the constant availability of the directional pull of gravity, used by the tree to find the direction of its growth); in which deadly foes are threatening (that is, in which crucially significant objects exist for visual identification); and in which escape is possible if these foes are identified *at a sufficient distance.*

14.   All this adaptation is of the nature of long-term knowledge about the environment. And a little thinking will make it clear that without this kind of adaptation, without this kind of knowledge of law-like regularities, sense organs like the eyes would be useless. Thus we must conclude that the eyes could never have evolved without an unconscious and very rich knowledge about long-term environmental conditions. This knowledge, no doubt, evolved together

with the eyes and with their use. Yet at every step it must have somehow preceded the evolution of the sense organ, and of its use. For the knowledge of the pre-conditions of its use are built into the organ.

15. Philosophers and even scientists often assume that all our knowledge stems from our senses, the 'sense data' which our senses deliver to us. They believe (as did, for example, the famous theorist of knowledge, Rudolf Carnap) that the question 'How do you know?' is in every case equivalent to the question 'What are the *observations* that entitle you to your assertion?'. But seen from a biological point of view, this kind of approach is a colossal mistake. For our senses to tell us anything, we must have *prior* knowledge. In order to be able to see a thing, we must know what 'things' are: that they can be located within some space; that some of them can move while others cannot; that some of them are of immediate importance to us, and there- fore are noticeable and will be noticed, while others, less important, will never penetrate into our consciousness: they may not even be unconsciously noticed, but they may simply leave no trace whatever upon our biological apparatus. For this apparatus is highly active and selective, and it actively selects only what is at the moment of biological importance. But in order to do so, it must be able to use adaptation, expectation: prior knowledge of the situation must be available, including its possibly significant elements. This prior knowledge cannot, in turn, be the result of observa- tion; it must, rather, be the result of an evolution by trial and error. Thus the eye itself is not the result of observation, but the result of evolution by trial and error, of adaptation, of non-observational long-term knowledge. And it is the result of such knowledge, derived not from short-term observation, but from adaptation to the environment and to such situations as constitute the *problems to be solved in the task of living*; situations that make our organs, among them our sense organs, significant instruments in the moment-by- moment task of living.

16. I hope I have been able to give you some idea of the importance of the distinction between long-term and short-term adaptation, long-term and short-term knowledge, and of the fundamental character of the long-term knowledge: of the fact that it must always precede short-term or observational knowledge, and of the impossibility that long-term knowledge can be obtained from short-term knowledge alone. Also, I hope that I have been able to show you that both kinds of knowledge are hypothetical: both are conjectural knowledge, although in a different way. (Our knowledge, or a tree's knowledge, of gravity will turn out to be gravely mistaken if we, or the tree, are placed in a no-longer accelerated rocket or ballistic missile.) Long-term conditions (and the knowledge of them) may be subject to revision; and an instance of short-term knowledge may turn out to be a misinterpretation.

And so we come to the decisive and perhaps most general proposition, valid for all organisms including man, even though it may perhaps not cover all forms of human knowledge.

17. All adaptations to environmental and to internal regularities, to long-term situations and to short-term situations, are kinds of knowledge – kinds of knowledge whose great importance we can learn from evolutionary biology. There are, perhaps, some forms of human knowledge that are not, or not obviously, forms of adaptations, or of attempted adaptations. But, roughly speaking, almost all forms of knowledge of an organism, from the unicellular amoeba to Albert Einstein, serve the organism to adapt itself to its actual tasks, or to tasks that may turn up in the future.

18. Life can only exist, and can only survive, if it is in some degree adapted to its environment. We can thus say that knowledge – primitive knowledge, of course – is as old as life. It originated together with the origin of pre-cellular

life, more than three thousand eight hundred million years ago. (Unicellular life came into existence not much later.) This happened soon after the earth cooled down sufficiently to allow some of the water in its atmosphere to liquify. Until then, water had existed only in the form of steam or clouds, but now hot liquid water began to collect in rocky basins, big or small, forming the first rivers, lakes, and seas.

19. Thus, the origin and the evolution of knowledge may be said to coincide with the origin and the evolution of life, and to be closely linked with the origin and evolution of our planet earth. Evolutionary theory links knowledge, and with it ourselves, with the cosmos; and so the problem of knowledge becomes a problem of cosmology.

Here I end my list of some of the conclusions that can be drawn from the proposition that animals can have knowledge.

I may perhaps very briefly refer to my book, *The Logic of Scientific Discovery*, first published in German in 1934, and published in English for the first time 25 years later, in 1959. In the Preface to the first English edition I wrote of the fascination of the *problem of cosmology*; and I said of it: 'It is the problem of understanding the world – including ourselves, and our knowledge, as part of the world.'

This is how I still see the setting of the evolutionary theory of knowledge.

When our solar system evolved and the earth had cooled sufficiently, there must have developed conditions in some place on earth that were favourable to the origin and to the evolution of life. Unicellular bacterial life quickly spread all over the earth. But those originally so very favourable local conditions could hardly have prevailed over many different geographical regions; so it seems that life must have had a struggle. Yet, in a comparatively short time, many different bacterial forms evolved that were adapted to very different environmental conditions.

Such, it appears, are the facts. Of course, they are far from certain: they are hypothetical interpretations of some geological findings. But if they are even approximately correct, they refute, for two reasons, the at present most widely accepted theory of the origin of life: the so-called 'soup theory' or 'broth theory'.

First reason: as the leading defenders of the soup theory assert, this theory demands a low temperature for the soup or broth in which the macromolecules develop, and later join up to form the first organism. The reason for their assertion is that, if the temperature is not very low (the broth must be considerably supercooled below 0°C), the macromolecules quickly decompose, instead of joining up.

But what we know of the earth in those days indicates that no such cool places existed. The surface of the earth, and even more the seas, were much hotter than today; and even today a watering place supercooled below 0°C would not easily be available, except perhaps near the North Pole or within a refrigerating plant.

Second reason: the theory that the macromolecules in the soup have joined up, and so have organized themselves into a living organism, is improbable in the extreme. The improbability is so great that one would have to assume an extremely long time-span in order to make the event a little less improbable; a time-span far longer, indeed, than the calculated time for which the cosmos has existed. So say even some of the most prominent defenders of the soup theory.

This constitutes a sound refutation of the theory in question, for as geologists found, the time-span between the formation of (boiling hot) liquid water and the origin of life is surprisingly short, and far too short to allow for an event of such extreme improbability to happen – even if the high temperature were acceptable to the soup theorists.

These two reasons constitute two refutations of the at present ruling soup theory of the origin of life. (There are many other refutations.) It is therefore fortunate that an alternative theory was published in 1988, a theory which is not beset by these or by similar difficulties. It assumes only the existence of such simple inorganic micromolecules as those of water, iron, carbon dioxide and hydrosulphide. No organic macromolecules are assumed to be present before the first metabolic cycles start and, with them, the chemical self-organizing of life. The new theory shows in detail how organic molecules (such as sugar) may evolve in time, perhaps deep down in the sea, bound to the surface of pyrite crystals, rather than in a solution. The anaerobic formation of the pyrite crystal creates the free chemical energy needed for the chemical processes – especially carbon fixation – that constitute the earliest form of pre-cellular life.

This new theory of the origin of life has been developed by its author in considerable detail, and it seems to be very successful: it explains many biochemical pathways. It is readily testable by experiments. But its greatest strength is that it can explain many biochemical facts that were unexplained before.

Günter Wächtershäuser, the author of this new biochemical theory, has also provided another biochemical theory – one that is of still greater relevance to the evolutionary theory of knowledge and to the problems we are discussing here. He has produced a biochemical theory of the origin of the first light-sensitive organ; that is, of the earliest evolutionary predecessor of our eyes. Since our eyes are our most important sense organs, this result is of great interest to our discussion.

The main result is this. It is known that some early uni-cellular micro-organism, presumably a bacterium, invented a revolutionary electro-chemical method of transforming sunlight into chemical energy: a method of using sunlight as a food, a method of feeding on sunlight. It was a bold and, indeed, a dangerous invention since, as we all know, too much sunlight – and especially the ultraviolet portion of sunlight – can kill. So with this invention, several problems arose for the cell (that previously may have been living deep down in the dark sea). They were pointed out by Wächtershäuser.

The first problem was to find out *where* sunlight is and, by using this information, to move towards it. This problem was solved by the first formation of a sense organ with the function of our eyes, a sense organ chemically linked to some already existing executive mechanism for the move-ment of the cell.

A second problem that arose was that of avoiding the danger of getting too much ultraviolet sunlight: of moving away in time, before suffering damage, towards some shade, presumably towards a deeper layer of sea water.

Thus in the evolution of the eye, even its earliest predecessor had to become *a controller of the movement of the cell*. It had to become part of the feeding mechanism of the cell, and part of its security movements: its mechanism for evading danger. The eye helped to avoid radiation damage to the cell – to anticipate danger. Even its very first function assumed prior knowledge of environmental states and possibilities.

Wächtershäuser pointed out that the revolutionary inven-tion of feeding on sunlight would have been self-destructive without that other, that essentially protective invention of moving out of sunlight (and presumably also into it) becom-ing part of the invention of the early eye and its link to the apparatus of motion. And so the problem arises in his theory: how could these two great inventions come together?

If we take an interest in biological evolution, especially in early evolution, then we must be constantly aware of the fact that life is, basically, a chemical *process*. It was Heraclitus, half a millenium before the birth of Christ, who said that life was a process, like fire; and, indeed, our life is something like a complex process of chemical oxidation. In the earliest stages of its evolution, when free oxygen was not available, sulphur played its role instead. As you may know, it was the bacterial invention of using sunlight as food – which, incidentally, led later to the self-invention of the kingdom of plants – that produced the greatest of all life-induced revolutions in the history of our environment: it introduced oxygen into the atmosphere. And so it created the air that we know, that makes *our* life possible, life as we know it: *our* breathing, *our* lungs, *our* fire (within and without). Heraclitus was right: we are not things, but flames. Or a little more prosaically, we are, like all cells, *processes of metabolism*; nets of chemical processes, of highly active (energy-coupled) chemical pathways.

The great Belgian biochemist Marcel Florkin (1900–1979) was one of the first to see clearly that *the evolution of life, or organisms, is an evolution of nets of chemical pathways*. The net of pathways that constitutes a cell at some given period of time may make it possible for some *new* pathway, often just a slight variation, to graft itself upon the then extant system. The new pathway may have been impossible without some of the chemical compounds produced by the old system of pathways. As Florkin pointed out, the net of chemical pathways of an extant cell often still retains, as part of this net, the archaic pathways of some billion years ago that made the later graftings possible. This, as Florkin pointed out, is analogous to the way in which anatomic pathways of the anatomic construction of the developing embryo may still retain those of its archaic ancestors of, say, some hundred million years ago. Thus the extant pathways of the metabolism may reveal some of its evolutionary history; a situation analogous to the so-called 'biogenetic law' of Fritz Müller and Ernst Haeckel.

It is within this setting of Florkin's ideas that Wächtershäuser was able to explain the riddle of the coincidence of the two great inventions: the invention of feeding on sunlight and the invention of light-sensitivity, of the archaic eye. The explanation is that both inventions are chemically very closely related: one of the pathways producing the machinery for feeding on sunlight and the pathway for producing the visual apparatus are structurally connected.

We may speculate that the invention resulted from the general tendency of organisms to explore their environment; in this case, by rising towards the surface layer of the sea. Presumably, the one or the other of these bacteria had, accidentally, evolved to a stage that made it possible to invent both of these new, chemically connected, grafts. Other organisms will also have boldly ventured near the surface, only to be destroyed by sunlight. But one (or perhaps a few) had the right chemical outfit, and survived. It was able to turn the surface layer of the sea into the richest feeding ground for its offspring; and its offspring exuded those huge amounts of oxygen that transformed the atmosphere.

We see that the Darwinian trial-and-error method turns out to be a method of the (partly accidental) variation and accretion of chemical pathways. In extant cells the pathways are controlled, step by chemical step, by enzymes which are highly specific chemical catalysts, that is, chemical means of speeding up specific chemical steps; and the enzymes are partly controlled by the genes. But a genetic mutation, and the synthesis of a new enzyme, will not lead to a new step in the net of pathways unless the new enzyme accidentally fits into the extant net; it is always the existing structure of the net of pathways that determines what new variations or accretions are possible. It is the existing net that contains the potentiality for new inventions; and a fitting enzyme, if not yet available, may become available soon. In some cases it may decide the future evolution of the species by determining which of the potential steps will be realized. (One step may lead to a slow evolution while another step may lead to a cascade of further steps. Both steps will be equally Darwinian, since they are subject to selection; their apparently different speeds are likely to be explicable in chemical terms.)

I will now try to list some of the lessons to be learned for the theory of knowledge from all that has been said so far.

The main lesson to be drawn may be formulated, perhaps with some little exaggeration, as follows. Even in the most primitive organisms, and even in the most primitive cases of sensitivity, everything depends upon the organism itself: upon its structure, its state, its activity. More especially, even if we confine our discussion for the moment to the problem of obtaining some knowledge from the environment with the help of the organism's sensitivity to the momentary state of its environment, even then everything will depend on the organism's own state, its long-term structure, its state of preparation for solving its problems, its state of activity.

In order to develop more fully what I have just said only very roughly, it is useful to introduce here a variant of the Kantian terminology of *a priori* and *a posteriori*. In Kant, knowledge *a priori* means knowledge that we possess *prior* to sense-observation; and knowledge *a posteriori* means knowledge we possess *posterior* to sense-observation, or after observation; and I will use the terms '*a priori*' and '*a posteriori*' only in this temporal or historical sense. (Kant himself uses his term *a priori* to mean, in addition, knowledge that is not merely prior to observation but also '*a priori* valid'; by which he means necessarily or certainly true. Of course, I shall not follow him in this since I am stressing the uncertain and conjectural character of our knowledge.) So I shall use the term 'a priori' to characterize that kind of knowledge – of fallible or conjectural knowledge – which an organism has *prior to sense experience*; roughly speaking, it is *inborn* knowledge. And I shall use the term '*a posteriori*' for knowledge that is obtained with the help of the sensitivity of the organism to momentary changes in the state of its environment.

Using this Kantian terminology with the modifications I have just indicated, we can now say that Kant's own position – highly revolutionary at the time – is this.

(A)   Most knowledge of detail, of the momentary state of our surroundings, is *a posteriori*.

(B)   But such *a posteriori* knowledge is impossible without *a priori* knowledge that we somehow *must* possess before we can acquire observational or *a posteriori* knowledge: without it, *what our senses tell us can make no sense*. We must establish an overall frame of reference, or else there will be no context available to make sense of our sensations.

(C)   This *a priori* knowledge contains, especially, knowledge of the structure of space and time (of space and time relations), and of causality (of causal relations).

I think that, in all these points, Kant is right. (Incidentally, I also think that he had hardly a real successor in this except perhaps Schopenhauer.) In my opinion, Kant anticipated the most important results of the evolutionary theory of knowledge.

But I am going much further than Kant. I think that, say, 99 per cent of the knowledge of all organisms is inborn and incorporated in our biochemical constitution. And I think that 99 per cent of the knowledge taken by Kant to be *a posteriori* and to be '*data*' that are 'given' to us through our senses is, in fact, not *a posteriori*, but *a priori*. For our senses can serve us (as Kant himself saw) only with yes-and-no answers to our own questions; questions that we conceive, and ask, *a priori*; and questions that sometimes are very elaborate. Moreover, even the yes-and-no answers of the senses have to be *interpreted* by us – interpreted in the light of our *a priori* preconceived ideas. And, of course, they are often *misinterpreted*.

Thus, all our knowledge is hypothetical. It is an adaptation to a partly unknown environment. It is often successful and often unsuccessful, the result of anticipatory trials and of unavoidable errors, *and of error elimination*. Some of the errors that have entered the inheritable constitution of an organism are eliminated by eliminating their bearer; that is, the individual organism. But some errors escape, and this is one reason why we are all fallible: our adaptation to the environment is never optimal, and it is always imperfect. A frog is constituted *a priori* so that it can see its prey – a fly – only when the fly moves. When the fly sits still, the frog cannot see it, even if it is very close: the frog's adaptation is imperfect.

Organisms and their organs incorporate expectations about their environment; and expectations – as we have seen – are homologous with our theories: as homologous as is the nose of my dog with my nose. So I suggest the hypothesis that adaptations and expectations are homologous even with *scientific theories* (and *vice versa* theories with adaptations and expectations). Theories may often contain evaluations. A unicellular organism's sensitivity to light, to heat, and to acidity may help it to escape from too little or too much of any of these. The organism's structure may incorporate the theory: 'the surrounding water can be dangerous: it may be too hot or too cold, and it may be too much or too little acid.' Clearly, such evaluations can evolve only if the organism is *able to take action*; for example, by moving away if it anticipates danger from these environmental states. Problems, values, and activity all evolve together.

I have said something about the origin of the archaic eye; and we can now say that its invention incorporates new discoveries, new theories, new knowledge about the environment and also the possibility of new values. For the first bacterium that not only achieved the new chemical synthesis, but went with it to a layer near the surface of the sea and survived, after millions of its brothers had succumbed, proved by its survival that it had solved a *problem* of adaptation; and in solving a *problem*, it introduced a new theory about new *values*. The invention was incorporated in the structure of the organism; in new, inheritable knowledge and therefore in new *a priori* knowledge.

Within this great revolution, the momentary signals conveyed by the eye to the organism were as such comparatively unimportant. They became important only together with the state of the organism; say, its need for food. The eye certainly helped the organism to feed on sunrays without destruction. But signals as such that, by homology, we might call the 'data' need not even be noticed. What leads to action are the *interpreted* signals (and interpretation is part of the action): signals *plus* the new theoretical evaluation of advantages and of danger; not objective 'data', but enticements and warnings acquired and *interpreted* with the help of the *a priori* structure of the organism.

We have seen that, even in bacteria, theories or hypotheses come before the signals, the 'sensations'. I need hardly stress that, especially in science, hypotheses come *before* what some scientists still call the 'data'; misleadingly, because they are not *given* to us, but actively (and sometimes at great peril) *sought and acquired* by us.

Observations (or 'data') may lead in science to the *abandonment* of a scientific theory and thereby induce some of us to think up a new tentative theory – a new trial. But the new theory is *our* product, *our* thought, *our* invention; and a new theory is only rarely thought up by more than a few people, even when there are many who agree on the refutation of the old theory. The few are those who *see the new problem*. Seeing a new problem may well be the most difficult step in creating a new theory.

The invention of the eye is thus an invention of new theoretical *a priori* knowledge, of an adaptation to the environment. It was from the first an adaptation to a long-term environmental structure: to the existence of potentially edible sunlight; it thus incorporates knowledge of this environmental structure. It is theoretical knowledge of a high degree of universality, almost like Kantian knowledge of space and time. It creates the possibility of momentary 'observation' or, more precisely, of the adaptation to a momentary situation of the environment. It may induce in the organism states of enticement or of repulsion, and it may make possible the release of prepared actions upon the environment. Thus, the invention of a highly universal theory (in this case the invention of a sense organ) may come before the observation (the use of the sense organ): it makes observation possible and introduces it into the set of actions that are available to the organism. And so it is itself an adaptation, found by trial and error. Theories (scientific or otherwise) are trials, inventions; they are *not* the results of many observations; they are *not* derived from many data.

Clearly, the first invention of the eye was a great achievement. Much of it has been preserved, and much evolved further. And yet, we – in common with all animals – have forgotten the knowledge that sunlight is edible, and how to eat it. And to this day we have not fully regained this knowledge.

Ladies and Gentlemen, I am one of those who love science and who think that science is enlightened common sense. I even think it is not much more than enlightened bacterial common sense! This is a view that, admittedly, clashes with common sense; but I hope that I have shown in this lecture that it need not clash with *enlightened* common sense. I have, I believe, refuted classical empiricism – the bucket theory of the mind that says that we obtain knowledge just by opening our eyes and letting the sense-given or god-given 'data' stream into a brain that will digest them.

Christopher Isherwood expressed this view by the title of his book, *I am a Camera*. But when he chose this title he forgot that even a camera must have an *a priori* built-in constitution; that there are primitive cameras and surprisingly evolved ones; and that in a failing light in which a bad camera records nothing, a good camera may produce a perfect picture, giving us all we want of it. It is better adapted to the environment, and also to our needs, that is, to our problems: it incorporates certain values that we have evolved while working on the evolution of the camera. But a lot of things it cannot do; for example, it cannot improve itself; and it cannot invent a new important problem, or a new tentative solution.

All organisms are problem finders and problem solvers. And all problem solving involves evaluations and, with it, values. Only with life do problems and values enter the world. And I do not believe that computers will ever invent important new problems, or new values.

Of these new values that we have invented, two seem to me the most important for the evolution of knowledge: a self-critical attitude – a value that we should always teach ourselves to live up to; and truth – a value that we should always seek our theories to live up to.

The first of these values, a self-critical attitude, first enters the world with objective products of life, such as spiders' webs, birds' nests, or beaver dams: products that can be repaired or improved. The emergence of the self-critical attitude is the beginning of something even more important:

of *the critical approach*, an approach that is critical in the interest of *objective truth*. (I hope that it was the critical approach that inspired the Founders of the London School of Economics to choose the dam-repairing beaver for its coat of arms.)

Both of these values, the critical approach and objective truth, enter our world only with the human language, the first and most important product of the human mind. Language makes it possible to consider our theories critically: to look at them as if they were external objects, as if they belonged to the world outside of ourselves which we share with others. Theories become objects of criticism, like the beaver dam. And we can try to repair them in the light of that most important value: correspondence to the facts – *truth*.

I have often said that from the amoeba to Einstein there is only one step. Both work with the method of trial and error. The amoeba must hate error, for it dies when it errs. But Einstein knows that we can learn only from our mistakes, and he spares no effort to make new trials in order to detect new errors, and to eliminate them from our theories. The step that the amoeba cannot take, but Einstein can, is to achieve a critical, a self-critical attitude, a critical approach. It is the greatest of the virtues that the invention of the human language puts within our grasp. I believe that it will make peace possible.

Let me end with a quotation from Albrecht Dürer, an artist and a scientist:

But I shall let the little I have learnt go forth into the day in order that someone better than I may guess the truth, and in his work may prove and rebuke my error. At this I shall rejoice that I was yet the means whereby this truth has come to light.